About the Author

Murat Durmus is CEO and founder of AISOMA (a Frankfurt am Main (Germany) based company specialized in AI-based technology development and consulting) and Author of the books THE AI THOUGHT BOOK & INSIDE ALAN TURING.

You can get in touch with the Author via:

- LinkedIn: https://www.linkedin.com/in/ceosaisoma/
- E-Mail: murat.durmus@aisoma.de

Background Image (Cover): Flickr - Björn Hermans - Mauve flower covered with small rain drops (https://www.flickr.com/photos/bhermans/624127366)

Ornament: Flickr - margot3001 - https://pixabay.com/de/vectors/ornament-dekorative-figur-gestaltung-1874436/

Rumi Portrait: http://rumiurdu.blogspot.com/p/about-masnavi.html

RUMI

Drops

of

Enlightenment

(Quotes & Poems)

Murat Durmus

*"You are not a drop in the ocean.
You are the entire ocean in a drop."*

~ Rumi

FOREWORD

1

INTRODUCTION

3

RUMI

13

RUMI TIMELINE

77

RECOMMENDED READINGS ON RUMI

81

FOREWORD

I remember it well as if it were yesterday. I was ten years old when my father took me to a performance of the dancing dervishes in Konya. I was fascinated by the elegance of their movements as if they were floating. But, to be honest, I did not know how to classify my impressions at that moment. It was just too much. On the one hand, I was deeply impressed and touched; on the other hand, I was afraid (today, I would call it awe). In any case, my visit at that time left lasting impressions. So much so that they keep coming back to my mind.

Rumi's poems and quotations are omnipresent. They appear everywhere and one cannot escape their depth, beauty and meaning. They are a part of great human creativity and remind us repeatedly how powerful (in a positive sense) words can be.

This little booklet is addressed to all who believe in beauty, love, mindfulness and the power of words. May Rumi's words touch you as they have always touched me and be a companion for a fulfilling and inspiring life.

Murat Durmus
13 March 2022, Frankfurt am Main (Germany)

INTRODUCTION

Jalal ad-Din Muhammad Rumi

Jalāl al-Dīn Muḥammad Rūmī (Persian: جلالالدین محمد رومی), (also known as Jalāl al-Dīn Muḥammad Balkhī (جلالدین محمد بلخی), Mevlânâ/Mawlānā (مولانا, "our master"), Mevlevî/Mawlawī (مولوی, "my master"), better known as Rumi (30. September 1207 - December 17, 1273), was a 13th-century Persian poet, Hanafite fajih, Islamic scholar, Maturide theologian, and Sufi mystic originally from Greater Khorasan in Greater Iran. Rumi's influence transcends national boundaries and ethnic divisions: Iranians, Tajiks, Turks, Greeks, Pashtuns, other Central Asian Muslims, and the Muslims of the Indian subcontinent have greatly appreciated his spiritual legacy over the past seven centuries. His poems have been translated into many languages of the world and translated into various formats. Rumi has been called the "most popular poet" and the "best-selling poet" in the United States.

Rumi's works are written primarily in Persian, but he occasionally used Turkish, Arabic, and Greek in his verse. His Masnavi (Mathnawi), which he wrote in Konya, is considered one of the greatest poems in Persian. His works are now read throughout Greater Iran and the Persian-speaking world in their original language. Translations of his works are very popular, especially in Turkey, Azerbaijan, the United States, and South Asia. His poems have influenced not only Persian literature but also the literary traditions of Ottoman Turkish, Chagatai, Urdu, Bengali, and Pashto.

(23 meters high statue of Mevlana in Buca, İzmir, Turkey[1])

---

[1] "23 meters high statue of Mevlana in Buca, İzmir, Turkey" Wikipedia, Faik Sarıkaya / wowTURKEY.com - Originally uploaded to www.wowturkey.com, https://en.wikipedia.org/wiki/Rumi#/media/File:Mevlana_Statue,_Buca.jpg.

Life

His father, Baha'uddin Walad, was a distinguished Persian-speaking preacher, jurist, and Sufi from Balch, whose spiritual lineage is also traced back to Ahmad Ghazali. His paternal grandfather, Hussein, was a noted scholar. According to an early biography, his paternal lineage traced back to Caliph Abu Bakr. In contrast, his mother, Mu'mineh, was the daughter of Muhammad Shah of Khwarism, the ruler of Khorasan.

Childhood and Youth

When Maulana (Rumi) was a child, the Mongols under Genghis Khan invaded Balkh in 1219; his father had foreseen this because the Khwarezmshah had some merchants of the Mongols killed and an act of revenge was to be feared. So, he and his family had already left the area to pilgrimage to Mecca. On the way, they met the famous Persian Sufi Fariduddin Attar in Naishapur, who was already an older man at that time.

Following the pilgrimage to Mecca, the family set out for Anatolia. During a stay in Laranda, today's Karaman, Jalal ad-Din's mother died. Her grave remains a place of pilgrimage to this day. Jalal ad-Din also married his wife Gauhar Chatun, a refugee from the East like him.

Education

The Seljuk sultan, Alā ed-Dīn Key-Qobād, who ruled the nearby city of Konya, heard of Baha'uddin Walad's new abode in 1228. Because he valued and encouraged the sciences and philosophy, he wrote to him to offer him a residence and a chair at the madrasa (university) of Konya. Maulana Jalal ad-Din Balchi (Rumi) studied Islamic sciences under his father and took over his chair after his death in 1230 or 1231.

The Mysticism

He was introduced to Sufism by a murshid named Sayyid Burhanuddin Muhaqqiq Tirmidhi. Together they traveled to Aleppo and Damascus, where they have met Ibn Arabi of Spain (Murcia), an influential Sufi master.

As a scholar, Maulana Jalal ad-Din (Rumi) achieved great fame, and he lived and acted as traditionally befitted a seasoned and highly respected scholar. However, when he met the dervish Shams-i Tabrizi (also known as Shamsuddin Tabrizi) in Konya in 1244, his life changed radically. Shams-i Tabriz was himself a disciple of Haci Bektas Veli, who lived simultaneously. The latter was a strong personality endowed with extraordinary spiritual abilities. The spiritual bond between the two friends became so intense that Maulana (Rumi) temporarily abandoned the world to devote himself entirely to his friend's secrets.

(An Ottoman era manuscript depicting Rumi and Shams-e Tabrizi.[2])

After the jealousy and envy of many influential people of Konya became too great, Shams fled the city. Rumi's grief was great until one day Shams returned. Probably because the situation became unbearable after some time, Shams then disappeared forever. It is assumed today that he was murdered. However, the longing for the friend inspired Maulana Jalal ad-Din (Rumi) to the rice dance, which is still imitated today, and to the poetry of his verses, which are also often quoted until today.

---

[2] "An Ottoman era manuscript depicting Rumi and Shams-e Tabrizi" Wikipedia, Unknown author - Topkapi Palace Museum, https://en.wikipedia.org/wiki/Rumi#/media/File:Meeting_of_Jalal_al-Din_Rumi_and_Molla_Shams_al-Din.jpg.

Works

After losing his friend Shams, Maulana (Rumi) repeatedly composed verses expressing his grief. His poetry, especially his 25,700 verse line poem Mathnawi (Turkish. Mesnevi), contains some of the most beautiful mystical verses ever written. It is also said of Maulana, "He is not a prophet, but he has a book," and that book, the Masnawi (Mathnawi), is also called the "Koran in Persian." Another major work of Maulana is the Diwan-i Shams-i Tabrizi (The Diwan of Shams-e Tabrizi; Shams-ad Din = Sun of Faith), which contains 35,000 lines. It was written over 30 years, from the disappearance of Shams to Maulana's death in Konya in 1273. Compared to the more sober Mathnawi, the Diwan more clearly reflects the feeling of mystical drunkenness.

Comparable to the Mathnawi is the prose collection Fihi ma fihi (On Being and Not Being). He gave these lectures to his disciples, just like Madschalis-i Sab'a (Seven Sessions), which he gave to the public before his meeting with Shams.

Of exclusively historical importance is his last work Makatib (Letters), for the most part, letters of recommendation in Persian to princes and nobles for the benefit of friends and disciples.

Since Persian was Maulana's mother tongue, Persian is also the language of his best-known works. However, he wrote a tiny part of his love poetry, which was not combined into one piece at the time, in Turkish and Greek.

Teaching

Maulana's (Rumi's) teaching was based on the fact that he considered love to be the main force of the universe. More precisely, the universe is a harmonious whole in which each part is in a love relationship with all others, which in turn is directed solely to God and can only endure through his love.

Man, who is created as a part of this harmonious whole, can achieve harmony with himself and the universe only when he learns to love God. His love for God will enable him to love his fellow human beings and all things created by God.

Coming closer to God through love is the path to true fulfillment in life for Maulana, just as for most Sufis. The reason for his fame is that he could render this teaching in the poetry of unsurpassable beauty. He described the joy of coming closer to God with the same eloquence as the sorrow of being separated from God. Like other mystical poets, he referred to God as the Beloved and the human soul searching for God as the Lover.

"When Rumi died on December 17, 1273, Jews, Christians, followers of Sufism, and other Muslims wept for him. The inhabitants of Konya accompanied Rumi to his grave, which has remained an important place of pilgrimage to this day."

Mausoleum

(Tomb of Jalal ad-Din Muhammad Rumi; Mevlâna mausoleum; Konya, Turkey[3])

After his death, Maulana Jalal ad-Din was buried in a mausoleum, which served as a meeting place (tekke) for the Maulawi Order (Turkish: Mevlevi). This mausoleum has been the landmark of Konya ever since, and to this day, it serves as a place of pilgrimage for devout Muslims and the followers of Maulana. When Atatürk

---

[3] "Tomb of Jalal ad-Din Muhammad Rumi; Mevlâna mausoleum; Konya, Turkey" Wikipedia, Georges Jansoone (JoJan), https://de.wikipedia.org/wiki/Rumi_(Dichter)#/media/Datei:Turkey.Konya008.jpg.

banned public religious acts on September 2, 1925, the Mevlevi Order was also affected in the course of secularization. Nevertheless, the tomb of Jalal ad-Din did not lose its importance; this can be seen, among other things, in the fact that it is customary among the general population to buy small amulets in the shape of the tomb after visiting the mausoleum (which has been turned into a museum by the Turkish government).

RUMI

(30 September 1207 – 17 December 1273)

Your task is not to seek for love, but merely to seek and find all the barriers within yourself that you have built against it.

Out beyond ideas of wrongdoing

and rightdoing there is a field.

I'll meet you there.

When the soul lies down in that grass

the world is too full to talk about.

❧

The wound is the place where the Light enters you.

❧

Stop acting so small.

You are the universe in ecstatic motion.

❧

What you seek is seeking you.

❧

Yesterday I was clever, so I wanted to change the world. Today I am wise, so I am changing myself.

❧

Don't grieve. Anything you lose comes round in another form.

❧

The minute I heard my first love story,

I started looking for you,

not knowing how blind that was.

Lovers don't finally meet somewhere.

They're in each other all along.
(The Illuminated Rumi)

Dance, when you're broken open.

Dance, if you've torn the bandage off.

Dance in the middle of the fighting.

Dance in your blood.

Dance when you're perfectly free.

If you are irritated by every rub, how will your mirror be polished?

Don't be satisfied with stories, how things have gone with others.

Unfold your own myth.

You were born with wings,

why prefer to crawl through life?

※

When you do things from your soul,

you feel a river moving in you, a joy.

※

Forget safety.

Live where you fear to live.

Destroy your reputation.

Be notorious.

※

Knock,

and he'll open the door

Vanish,

and he'll make you shine like the sun

Fall,

and he'll raise you to the heavens

Become nothing,

and he'll turn you into everything.

❧

When I am with you, we stay up all night.

When you're not here, I can't go to sleep.

Praise God for those two insomnias!

And the difference between them.

❧

Raise your words, not voice.

It is rain that grows flowers, not thunder.

❧

My soul is from elsewhere,

I'm sure of that, and I intend to end up there.

❧

I want to see you.

Know your voice.

Recognize you when you

first come 'round the corner.

Sense your scent when I come

into a room you've just left.

Know the lift of your heel,

the glide of your foot.

Become familiar with the way

you purse your lips

then let them part,

just the slightest bit,

when I lean in to your space

and kiss you.

I want to know the joy

of how you whisper

"more"

Silence is the language of God,

all else is poor translation.

Sell your cleverness and buy bewilderment.
(Masnavi i Man'avi, the spiritual couplets of Maula)

In your light I learn how to love.

In your beauty, how to make poems.

You dance inside my chest where no-one sees you,

but sometimes I do,

and that sight becomes this art.

Ignore those that make you fearful and sad,

that degrade you back towards disease and death.

Everything in the universe is within you.

Ask all from yourself.

Where there is ruin, there is hope for a treasure

I want to sing like the birds' sing, not worrying about who hears or what they think.

Be grateful for whoever comes, because each has been sent as a guide from beyond.

Let yourself be drawn by the stronger pull of that which you truly love.

Goodbyes are only for those who love with their eyes. Because for those who love with heart and soul there is no such thing as separation.

Words are a pretext.

It is the inner bond that draws one person to another, not words.

There is a candle in your heart, ready to be kindled.

There is a void in your soul, ready to be filled.

You feel it, don't you?

Travel brings power and love back into your life.

Set your life on fire.

Seek those who fan your flames

Be empty of worrying.

Think of who created thought!

Why do you stay in prison?

When the door is so wide open?
(The Essential Rumi)

This being human is a guest house.

Every morning is a new arrival.

A joy, a depression, a meanness, some momentary awareness comes as an unexpected visitor...

Welcome and entertain them all.

Treat each guest honorably.

The dark thought, the shame, the malice, meet them at the door laughing, and invite them in.

Be grateful for whoever comes, because each has been sent as a guide from beyond.

Sorrow prepares you for joy.

It violently sweeps everything out of your house, so that new joy can find space to enter.

It shakes the yellow leaves from the bough of your heart, so that fresh, green leaves can grow in their place.

It pulls up the rotten roots, so that new roots hidden beneath have room to grow.

Whatever sorrow shakes from your heart, far better things will take their place.

※

Let the beauty we love be what we do.

There are hundreds of ways to kneel and kiss the ground.

※

I know you're tired but come, this is the way.

※

Be like the sun for grace and mercy.

Be like the night to cover others' faults.

Be like running water for generosity.

Be like death for rage and anger.

Be like the Earth for modesty. Appear as you are. Be as you appear.

※

Suffering is a gift.

In it is hidden mercy.

༄

A thousand half-loves must be forsaken to take one whole heart home.

༄

We come spinning out of nothingness, scattering stars like dust.

༄

Come, come, whoever you are.

Wanderer, worshiper, lover of leaving.

It doesn't matter.

Ours is not a caravan of despair.

Come, even if you have broken your vows a thousand times.

Come, yet again, come, come.

༄

This is love:

to fly toward a secret sky,

to cause a hundred veils to fall each moment.

First to let go of life.

Finally, to take a step without feet.

※

Two there are who are never satisfied -- the lover of the world and the lover of knowledge.

※

Be melting snow.

Wash yourself of yourself.

※

And you?

When will you begin that long journey into yourself?

※

Wherever you are, and whatever you do, be in love.

※

I have lived on the lip of insanity,

wanting to know reasons, knocking on a door.

It opens.

I've been knocking from the inside.

Respond to every call that excites your spirit.
(The Essential Rumi)

Let yourself be silently drawn by the strange pull of what you really love.

It will not lead you astray.

Take someone who doesn't keep score,

who's not looking to be richer, or afraid of losing,

who has not the slightest interest even in his own personality: he's free.

Sit, be still, and listen,

because you're drunk

and we're at

the edge of the roof

Either give me more wine or leave me alone.

You have to keep breaking your heart until it opens.

People want you to be happy.

Don't keep serving them your pain!

If you could untie your wings

and free your soul of jealousy,

you and everyone around you

would fly up like doves.

When you go through a hard period,

When everything seems to oppose you,

... when you feel you cannot even bear one more minute,

NEVER GIVE UP!

Because it is the time and place that the course will divert!

※

Start a huge, foolish project, like Noah...

it makes absolutely no difference what people think of you.

※

The cure for pain is in the pain.

※

Reason is powerless in the expression of Love.

※

But listen to me. For one moment quit being sad.

Hear blessings dropping their blossoms around you

※

I closed my mouth and spoke to you in a hundred silent ways.

※

What hurts you, blesses you. Darkness is your candle.

Study me as much as you like, you will not know me,

for I differ in a hundred ways from what you see me to be.

Put yourself behind my eyes and see me as I see myself, for I have chosen to dwell in a place you cannot see.

These pains you feel are messengers. Listen to them.

The breezes at dawn have secrets to tell you

Don't go back to sleep!

You must ask for what you really want.

Don't go back to sleep!

People are going back and forth

across the doorsill where the two worlds touch,

The door is round and open

Don't go back to sleep!

❦

A mountain keeps an echo deep inside.

That's how I hold your voice.

❦

That which God said to the rose, and caused it to laugh in full-blown beauty,

he said to my heart, and made it a hundred times more beautiful.

❦

You were born with potential.

You were born with goodness and trust. You were born with ideals and dreams. You were born with greatness.

You were born with wings.

You are not meant for crawling, so don't.

You have wings.

Learn to use them and fly.

Who could be so lucky?

Who comes to a lake for water and sees the reflection of moon?

You try to be faithful

And sometimes you're cruel.

You are mine. Then, you leave.

Without you, I can't cope.

And when you take the lead,

I become your footstep.

Your absence leaves a void.

Without you, I can't cope.

You have disturbed my sleep,

You have wrecked my image.

You have set me apart.

Without you, I can't cope.
(Love: The Joy That Wounds: The Love Poems of Rumi)

Oh soul,

you worry too much.

You have seen your own strength.

You have seen your own beauty.

You have seen your golden wings.

Of anything less,

why do you worry?

You are in truth the soul,

of the soul, of the soul.

You are not a drop in the ocean.

You are the entire ocean in a drop.

Christian, Jew, Muslim, Shaman, Zoroastrian, stone, ground, mountain, river, each has a secret way of being with the mystery, unique and not to be judged.

I choose to love you in silence…

For in silence, I find no rejection,

I choose to love you in loneliness…

For in loneliness no one owns you but me,

I choose to adore you from a distance…

For distance will shield me from pain,

I choose to kiss you in the wind…

For the wind is gentler than my lips,

I choose to hold you in my dreams…

For in my dreams, you have no end.

If you desire healing,

let yourself fall ill

let yourself fall ill.

You wander from room to room.

Hunting for the diamond necklace.

That is already around your neck!

Do you know what you are?

You are a manuscript of a divine letter.

You are a mirror reflecting a noble face.

This universe is not outside of you.

Look inside yourself;

everything that you want,

you are already that.

I didn't come here of my own accord,

and I can't leave that way.

Whoever brought me here will have to take me home.

Only from the heart can you touch the sky.

I was dead, then alive.

Weeping, then laughing.

The power of love came into me,

and I became fierce like a lion,

then tender like the evening star.

※

My heart is so small

it's almost invisible.

How can You place

such big sorrows in it?

Look," He answered,

your eyes are even smaller,

yet they behold the world.

※

Your hand opens and closes, opens and closes.

If it were always a fist or always stretched open,

you would be paralyzed.

Your deepest presence is in every small contracting and expanding,

the two as beautifully balanced and coordinated as birds' wings.
(The Essential Rumi)

※

In Silence there is eloquence.

Stop weaving and see how the pattern improves.

※

Run from what's comfortable. Forget safety.

Live where you fear to live.

Destroy your reputation.

Be notorious.

I have tried prudent planning long enough.

From now on I'll be mad.

※

An eye is meant to see things.

The soul is here for its own joy.

A head has one use: For loving a true love.

Feet: To chase after.

Love is for vanishing into the sky. The mind,

for learning what men have done and tried to do.

Mysteries are not to be solved:

The eye goes blind

when it only wants to see why.

A lover is always accused of something.

But when he finds his love, whatever was lost

in the looking comes back completely changed.
(Night and Sleep)

At night, I open the window

and ask the moon to come

and press its face against mine.

Breathe into me.

Close the language-door

and open the love-window.

The moon won't use the door,

only the window.

❦

You think because you understand 'one' you must also understand 'two',

because one and one make two. But you must also understand 'and'.

❦

The moon stays bright when it doesn't avoid the night.

❦

Be a lamp, or a lifeboat, or a ladder.

Help someone's soul heal.

Walk out of your house like a shepherd.

❦

Beauty surrounds us.

※

Like a sculptor, if necessary,

carve a friend out of stone.

Realize that your inner sight is blind

and try to see a treasure in everyone.

※

God turns you from one feeling to another and teaches by means of opposites so that you will have two wings to fly, not one.

※

Here is a relationship booster that is guaranteed to

work:

Every time your spouse or lover says something stupid

make your eyes light up as if you

just heard something

brilliant.

❦

Let the lover be disgraceful, crazy, absentminded.
Someone sober will worry about things going badly.
Let the lover be.

❦

Remember.

The way you make love is the way God will be with you.

❦

Inside you there's an artist you don't know about...
say yes quickly, if you know, if you've known it from before the beginning of the universe.

❦

Moonlight floods the whole sky from horizon to horizon;

How much it can fill your room depends on its windows.
(The Essential Rumi)

❦

I am your moon and your moonlight too

I am your flower garden and your water too

I have come all this way, eager for you

Without shoes or shawl

I want you to laugh

To kill all your worries

To love you

To nourish you

※

When you feel a peaceful joy,

that's when you are near truth.

※

Let the beauty of what you love be what you do.

※

On a day when the wind is perfect,

the sail just needs to open and the world is full of beauty.

Today is such a day.

❧

The breeze at dawn has secrets to tell you. Don't go back to sleep.

❧

Lovers find secret places inside this violent world where they make transactions with beauty.

❧

When someone is counting out gold for you, don't look at your hands, or the gold. Look at the giver.
(The Masnavi: Book Two)

❧

They say there is a doorway from heart to heart, but what is the use of a door when there are no walls?

❧

Put your thoughts to sleep, do not let them cast a shadow over the moon of your heart. Let go of thinking.

❧

There is a secret medicine given only to those who hurt so hard they can't hope.

The hopers would feel slighted if they knew.
(The Essential Rumi)

※

Anyone who knows me, should learn to know me again;

For I am like the Moon, you will see me with new face every day.

※

You are a volume in the divine book.

A mirror to the power that created the universe.

Whatever you want, ask it of yourself.

Whatever you're looking for can only be found

Inside of you.

※

I will soothe you and heal you,

I will bring you roses.

I too have been covered with thorns.

※

Within tears, find hidden laughter.

Seek treasures amid ruins, sincere one.

※

Give up to grace. The ocean takes care of each wave 'til it gets to shore. You need more help than you know

※

For ages you have come and gone

courting this delusion.

For ages you have run from the pain

and forfeited the ecstasy.

So come, return to the root of the root

of your own soul.

Although you appear in earthly form

Your essence is pure Consciousness.

You are the fearless guardian

of Divine Light.

So come, return to the root of the root

of your own soul.

When you lose all sense of self

the bonds of a thousand chains will vanish.

Lose yourself completely,

Return to the root of the root

of your own soul.

You descended from Adam, by the pure Word of God,

but you turned your sight

to the empty show of this world.

Alas, how can you be satisfied with so little?

So come, return to the root of the root

of your own soul.

Why are you so enchanted by this world

when a mine of gold lies within you?

Open your eyes and come ---

Return to the root of the root

of your own soul.

You were born from the rays of God's Majesty

when the stars were in their perfect place.

How long will you suffer from the blows

of a nonexistent hand?

So come, return to the root of the root

of your own soul.

You are a ruby encased in granite.

How long will you deceive Us with this outer show?

O friend, we can see the truth in your eyes!

So come, return to the root of the root

of your own soul.

After one moment with that glorious Friend

you became loving, radiant, and ecstatic.

Your eyes were sweet and full of fire.

Come, return to the root of the root

of your own soul.

Shams-e Tabriz, the King of the Tavern

has handed you an eternal cup,

And God in all His glory is pouring the wine.

So, come! Drink!

Return to the root of the root

of your own soul.

Soul of all souls, life of all life - you are That.

Seen and unseen, moving and unmoving - you are That.

The road that leads to the city is endless;

Go without head and feet and you'll already be there.

What else could you be? - you are That

All people on the planet are children, except for a very few.

No one is grown up except those free of desire.

When someone beats a rug,

the blows are not against the rug,

but against the dust in it.

I once had a thousand desires. But in my one desire to know you all else melted away.

Do not feel lonely, the entire universe is inside you.

Is it really so that the one I love is everywhere?

There are lovers' content with longing.

I'm not one of them.

Like This

If anyone asks you

how the perfect satisfaction

of all our sexual wanting

will look, lift your face

and say,

Like this.

When someone mentions the gracefulness

of the nightsky, climb up on the roof

and dance and say,

Like this.

If anyone wants to know what "spirit" is,

or what "God's fragrance" means,

lean your head toward him or her.

Keep your face there close.

Like this.

When someone quotes the old poetic image

about clouds gradually uncovering the moon,

slowly loosen knot by knot the strings

of your robe.

Like this.

If anyone wonders how Jesus raised the dead,

don't try to explain the miracle.

Kiss me on the lips.

Like this. Like this.

> RUMI

When someone asks what it means

to "die for love," point

here.

If someone asks how tall I am, frown

and measure with your fingers the space

between the creases on your forehead.

This tall.

The soul sometimes leaves the body, the returns.

When someone doesn't believe that,

walk back into my house.

Like this.

When lovers moan,

they're telling our story.

Like this.

I am a sky where spirits live.

Stare into this deepening blue,

while the breeze says a secret.

Like this.

When someone asks what there is to do,

light the candle in his hand.

Like this.

How did Joseph's scent come to Jacob?

Huuuuu.

How did Jacob's sight return?

Huuuu.

A little wind cleans the eyes.

Like this.

When Shams comes back from Tabriz,

he'll put just his head around the edge

of the door to surprise us

Like this.

You think you are alive

because you breathe air?

Shame on you,

that you are alive in such a limited way.

Don't be without Love,

so, you won't feel dead.

Die in Love

and stay alive forever.

❧

The rose's rarest essence lives in the thorns.

❧

This place is a dream.

Only a sleeper considers it real.

Then death comes like dawn, and you wake up laughing at what you thought was your grief.

❧

My lips got lost on the way to the kiss

that's how drunk I was.

❧

"I will be waiting here....

For your silence to break,

For your soul to shake,

For your love to wake!
(The Essential Rumi)

❧

Somewhere beyond right and wrong, there is a garden. I will meet you there.

I searched for God among the Christians and on the Cross and therein I found Him not.

I went into the ancient temples of idolatry; no trace of Him was there.

I entered the mountain cave of Hira and then went as far as Qandhar but God I found not.

With set purpose I fared to the summit of Mount Caucasus and found there only 'anqa's habitation.

Then I directed my search to the Kaaba, the resort of old and young; God was not there even.

Turning to philosophy I inquired about him from ibn Sina but found Him not within his range.

I fared then to the scene of the Prophet's experience of a great divine manifestation only a "two bow-lengths' distance from him" but God was not there even in that exalted court.

Finally, I looked into my own heart and there I saw Him; He was nowhere else.

The lion is most handsome when looking for food.

※

Not only the thirsty seek the water, the water as well seeks the thirsty.

※

Gamble everything for love, if you're a true human being.

※

Shine like the whole universe is yours.

※

Maybe you are searching among the branches, for what only appears in the roots.

※

You are so weak. Give up to grace.

The ocean takes care of each wave till it gets to shore.

You need more help than you know.

※

The truth was a mirror in the hands of God. It fell, and broke into pieces. Everybody took a piece of it, and they looked at it and thought they had the truth.

You think of yourself

as a citizen of the universe.

You think you belong

to this world of dust and matter.

Out of this dust

you have created a personal image,

and have forgotten

about the essence of your true origin.

You have no idea how hard I've looked for a gift to bring You.

Nothing seemed right.

What's the point of bringing gold to the gold mine, or water to the ocean?

Everything I came up with was like taking spices to the Orient.

It's no good giving my heart and my soul because you already have these.

So, I've brought you a mirror. Look at yourself and remember me.

※

Drum sound rises on the air, its throb, my heart.

A voice inside the beat says,

"I know you're tired, but come. This is the way.

※

I said: what about my eyes?

He said: Keep them on the road.

I said: What about my passion?

He said: Keep it burning.

I said: What about my heart?

He said: Tell me what you hold inside it?

I said: Pain and sorrow.

He said: Stay with it. The wound is the place where the Light enters you.

What matters is how quickly you do what your soul directs.

Love comes with a knife, not some shy question, and not with fears for its reputation!

I am yours.

Don't give myself back to me.

Birds make great sky-circles of their freedom.

How do they learn it?

They fall and falling,

they're given wings.

Your heart is the size of an ocean. Go find yourself in its hidden depths.

Pain is a treasure, for it contains mercies.

Do not leave me,

hide in my heart like a secret,

wind around my head like a turban.

"I come and go as I please,"

you say, "swift as a heartbeat."

You can tease me as much as you like

but never leave me.

This is how I would die

into the love I have for you:

As pieces of cloud

dissolve in sunlight.

Keep walking, though there's no place to get to.

Don't try to see through the distances.

That's not for human beings. Move within,

But don't move the way fear makes you move.

❦

Whoever's calm and sensible is insane!

❦

Let silence take you to the core of life.

❦

Give your weakness to one who helps.

❦

She loved him so much she concealed his name in many phrases, the inner meanings known only to her.

❦

Sell your cleverness and buy bewilderment. Cleverness is mere opinion, bewilderment is intuition.

❦

Love calls - everywhere and always.

We're sky bound.

Are you coming?

The only lasting beauty is the beauty of the heart.

Try something different. Surrender.

Try not to resist the changes that come your way. Instead let life live through you.

And do not worry that your life is turning upside down.

How do you know that the side you are used to is better than the one to come?

I searched for God and found only myself.

I searched for myself and found only God.

Learn the alchemy true human beings know. The moment you accept what troubles you've been given the door with open.

The universe and the light of the stars come through me.

The ground's generosity takes in our compost and grows beauty!

Try to be more like the ground.

Listen with ears of tolerance!

See through the eyes of compassion!

Speak with the language of love.

Patience is not sitting and waiting, it is foreseeing.

It is looking at the thorn and seeing the rose, looking at the night and seeing the day.

Lovers are patient and know that the moon needs time to become full.

❦

Listen, O drop, give yourself up without regret,

and in exchange gain the Ocean.

Listen, O drop, bestow upon yourself this honor,

and in the arms of the Sea be secure.

Who indeed should be so fortunate?

An Ocean wooing a drop!

In God's name, in God's name, sell and buy at once!

Give a drop, and take this Sea full of pearls.

❦

The garden of the world has no limits,

except in your mind.

❦

You and I have spoken all these words, but for the way we have to go, words are no preparation. I have one small drop of knowing in my soul.

Let it dissolve in your ocean.

I am weary of personal worrying,

in love with the art of madness.

※

As you start to walk on the way, the way appears.

※

Look past your thoughts,

so you may drink the pure nectar of This Moment

※

Whenever we manage to love without expectations,

calculations, negotiations, we are indeed in heaven.

※

I am so close; I may look distant.

So completely mixed with you, I may look separate.

So out in the open, I appear hidden.

So silent, because I am constantly talking with you.

✦

Whatever purifies you is the right path,

I will not try to define it.

✦

The world's flattery and hypocrisy are a sweet morsel:

eat less of it, for it is full of fire.

Its fire is hidden while its taste is manifest,

but its smoke becomes visible in the end.

✦

You had better run from me.

My words are fire.

✦

Never lose hope, my heart, miracles dwell in the invisible.

If the whole world turns against you keep your eyes on the Friend.

✦

All day I think about it, then at night I say it.

Where did I come from, and what am I supposed to be doing?

I have no idea.

My soul is from elsewhere, I'm sure of that,

And I intend to end up there.

This drunkenness began in some other tavern.

When I get back around to that place,

I'll be completely sober. Meanwhile,

I'm like a bird from another continent, sitting in this aviary.

The day is coming when I fly off,

But who is it now in my ear who hears my voice?

Who says words with my mouth?

Who looks out with my eyes? What is the soul?

I cannot stop asking.

If I could taste one sip of an answer,

I could break out of this prison for drunks.

I didn't come here of my own accord, and I can't leave that way.

Whoever brought me here will have to take me home.

This poetry. I never know what I'm going to say.

I don't plan it.

When I'm outside the saying of it, I get very quiet and rarely speak at all.

We have a huge barrel of wine, but no cups.

That's fine with us. Every morning

We glow and, in the evening, we glow again

※

Where the lips are silent the heart has a thousand tongues.

※

If the foot of the trees were not tied to earth, they would be pursuing me.

For I have blossomed so much, I am the envy of the gardens.

※

I see my beauty in you.

Don't wait any longer.

Dive in the ocean,

Leave and let the sea be you.

※

Why do you stay in prison,

when the door is so wide open?

※

A Thirsty Fish

I don't get tired of you. Don't grow weary

of being compassionate toward me!

All this thirst equipment

must surely be tired of me,

the water jar, the water carrier.

I have a thirsty fish in me

that can never find enough

of what it's thirsty for!

Show me the way to the ocean!

Break these half-measures,

these small containers.

All this fantasy

and grief.

Let my house be drowned in the wave

that rose last night in the courtyard

hidden in the center of my chest.

Joseph fell like the moon into my well.

The harvest I expected was washed away.

But no matter.

> RUMI

A fire has risen above my tombstone hat.

I don't want learning, or dignity,

or respectability.

I want this music and this dawn

and the warmth of your cheek against mine.

The grief-armies assemble,

but I'm not going with them.

This is how it always is

when I finish a poem.

A great silence comes over me,

and I wonder why I ever thought

to use language.

❧

Have you ever gotten breathless before from a beautiful face,

for I see you there,

my dear.

❧

If the wine drinker

has a deep gentleness in him,

he will show that when drunk.

But if he has hidden anger and arrogance,

those appear.

❧

Everything you possess of skill, and wealth, and handicraft, wasn't it first merely a thought and a quest?

❧

Poems are rough notations for the music we are.

Something opens our wings.

Something makes boredom and hurt disappear.

Someone fills the cup in front of us: We taste only sacredness.

Love is the bridge between you and everything.

Your body is away from me,

but there is a window open

from my heart to yours.

Pull the thorn of existence out of the heart! Fast!

For when you do, you will see thousands of rose gardens in yourself.

Keep on knocking 'til the joy inside

opens a window look to see who's there.

✤

You have forgotten the One

who doesn't care about ownership,

who doesn't try to turn a profit

from every human exchange.

✤

Nothing can help me but that beauty.

There was a dawn I remember

when my soul heard something from your soul.

I drank water from your spring

and felt the current take me.

✤

Why struggle to open a door between us when the whole wall is an illusion?

✤

It's your road, and yours alone.

others may walk it with you,

but no one can walk it for you.

No more words. In the name of this place,

we drink in with our breathing,

stay quiet like a flower.

So, the nightbirds will start singing.

The art of knowing is knowing what to ignore.

Some nights stay up till dawn,

as the moon sometimes does for the sun.

Be a full bucket pulled up the dark way

of a well, then lifted out into light.

Love isn't the work of the tender and the gentle;

Love is the work of wrestlers.

The one who becomes a servant of lovers

is really a fortunate sovereign.

Don't ask anyone about Love; ask Love about Love.

Love is a cloud that scatters pearls

❦

Forget safety. Live where you fear to live.

❦

Woman is the light of God.

∞

RUMI TIMELINE

1207 - 1273

Life of the Persian poet Rumi, considered one of the greatest literary artists in the world.

c. 1215

Rumi's father flees Balkh, Afghanistan to escape invading Mongols; moves family to Konya, Anatolia.

c. 1228

Rumi is a highly-respected teacher and theologian living in Konya. When his father dies, he assumes his role as head of the religious community.

1244

Rumi meets the Sufi mystic Shams-i-Tabrizi and the two become inseparable friends.

1248

Shams-i-Tabrizi disappears; Rumi recognizes their spiritual connection is ongoing and begins to compose verse.

1248 - 1273

Rumi composes mystical poetry for the rest of his life, including his famous work, the Masnavi, still unfinished at the time of his death.[4]

---

[4] WORLD HISTORY ENCYCLOPEDIA:
https://www.worldhistory.org/timeline/Rumi/

RUMI TIMELINE

RECOMMENDED READINGS ON RUMI

- **The Essential Rumi (New Expanded Edition) by Coleman Barks**

This revised and expanded edition of The Essential Rumi includes a new introduction by Coleman Barks and more than 80 never-before-published poems.

(ISBN-13: 978-0062509598)

- **Rumi: The Book of Love by Coleman Barks**

This is the definitive collection of America's bestselling poet Rumi's finest poems of love and lovers. In Coleman Barks' delightful and wise renderings, these poems will open your heart and soul to the lover inside and out.

(ISBN-13: 978-0060750503)

- **The Masnavi, Book One (Oxford World's Classics) by Jawid Mojaddedi**

Rumi's Masnavi is widely recognized as the greatest Sufi poem ever written, and has been called "the Koran in Persian." The thirteenth-century Muslim mystic Rumi composed his work for the benefit of his disciples in the

Sufi order named after him, better known as the whirling dervishes.

(ISBN-13: 978-0199552313)

- **The Forty Rules of Love by Elif Shafak**

In this lyrical, exuberant tale, acclaimed Turkish author Elif Shafak, author of The Island of Missing Trees (a Reese's Book Club Pick), incarnates Rumi's timeless message of love

The Forty Rules of Love unfolds two tantalizing parallel narratives — one contemporary and the other set in the thirteenth century, when Rumi encountered his spiritual mentor, the whirling dervish known as Shams of Tabriz — that together explore the enduring power of Rumi's work.

(ISBN-13: 978-0143118527)

Also available on Amazon

KAHLIL GIBRAN

Boundless Sorrow & Unclouded Joy:

(Selected Quotes & Poems)

ISBN: 978-1471665950

"You talk when you cease to be at peace with your thoughts."

Made in United States
Troutdale, OR
11/07/2023